LOOK-ALIKES

SEEK-AND-SEARCH PUZZLES

L B

Little, Brown and Company
New York   Boston

JOAN STEINER

WHAT IS A LOOK-ALIKE?

When candy corn looks like a broom and thimbles look like buckets, you'll know you are in the Land of Look-Alikes! Your challenge is to find all the common, everyday objects pretending to be something else. HERE ARE SOME HINTS:

Nail clipper

Clothespin

Alphabet blocks

FIND THE **19** LOOK-ALIKES

Super Sleuth will tell you how many Look-Alikes are in each scene.
There are 19 here. Can you find them all?
The more you look, the more you see!

Now, for even more fun, we'll sneak in some changes. Some are easy to find, some are harder. The "spot" tells you that there are 4 changes in this one. CAN YOU FIND THEM?

THERE ARE ANSWERS IN THE BACK.
BUT NO PEEKING TILL YOU'VE TRIED!

FIND THE **37** LOOK-ALIKES

HOME SWEET HOME

TO SEARCH FOR LOOK-ALIKES, YOU NEED NOT ROAM.

THEY'RE ALL AROUND YOU— RIGHT HERE AT HOME.

Remember, these puzzles play tricks on your eyes.
Are you able to find these things in disguise?

 Tea bags

 Open book

 Brick

 Jigsaw pieces

 Pencil sharpener

 Whistle

 Dog biscuits

 Baby bottle nipple

 Peanuts

 Seashell

 Forks

 Wallet

BEDTIME BRAINTEASERS

Start in the bedroom, where you lay your head.

Is that a pillow . . . or is it bread?

FIND THE **40** LOOK-ALIKES

Which LOOK-ALIKES are toys?

PUZZLING PARLOR

This parlor's so cozy.
Pull up a seat.

And if you are hungry,
find good things to eat.

FIND THE **35** LOOK-ALIKES

Which LOOK-ALIKES can you eat
with tomato sauce?

KOOKY KITCHEN

If dinner's not ready
and the cupboard is bare,

You can snack on the Look-Alikes
and nibble your chair!

FIND THE **37** LOOK-ALIKES

Come sit by the fire,
come in from the cold,

As autumn leaves
turn to red and to gold.

FIND THE **28** LOOK-ALIKES

BONUS CHALLENGE

Things in this bathroom are not as they appear.

But at least the shower curtain is crystal clear!

A

B

C

D

FIND THE **14** LOOK-ALIKES

SPOT 2 THE SAME

IT'S TIME TO TACKLE A BONUS GAME– WHICH TWO ROOMS ARE EXACTLY THE SAME?

E

F

G

H

FIND THE 44 LOOK-ALIKES

IN MY NEIGHBORHOOD

NOW LOOK UP AND DOWN THIS STREET.

THERE ARE **LOOK-ALIKE** NEIGHBORS FOR YOU TO MEET.

To make sure that nothing will be missed,
This little girl brought a shopping list:

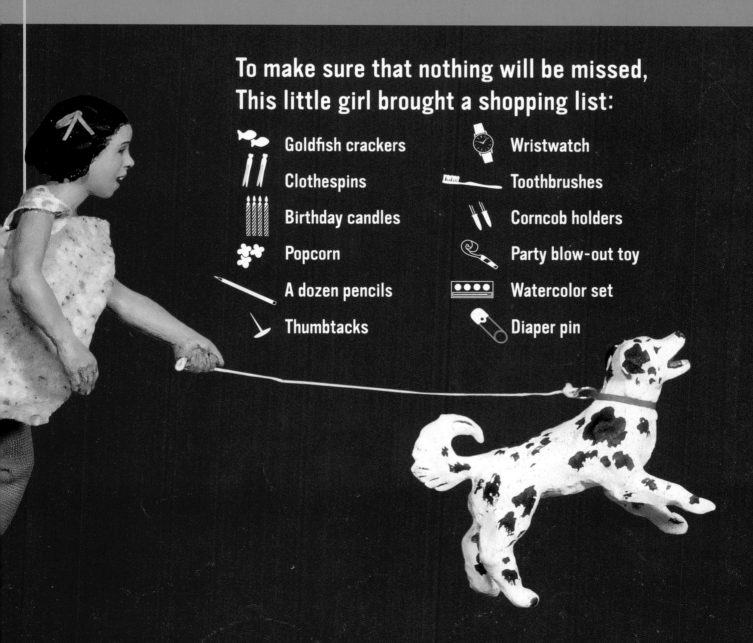

Goldfish crackers
Clothespins
Birthday candles
Popcorn
A dozen pencils
Thumbtacks

Wristwatch
Toothbrushes
Corncob holders
Party blow-out toy
Watercolor set
Diaper pin

CURIOUS CONSTRUCTION SITE

These apartments should all have musical keys,

When they finish this tower built of CDs.

FIND THE **43** LOOK-ALIKES

Which LOOK-ALIKES belong on a desk?

SCHOOLROOM SMARTS

At school you can hang your coat by the collar.

Can you see it?
It's right next to a dollar.

FIND THE **39** LOOK-ALIKES   Which LOOK-ALIKES start with the letter *P*?

DAFFY DINER

FIND THE **41** LOOK-ALIKES

Hanging out in a diner can be so cool,

Especially when you sit on a coin stool.

FIND THE **48** LOOK-ALIKES

The deli man's out
in the early morn'

To sweep the street
with candy corn.

BONUS CHALLENGE

SPOT **2** DIFFERENCES

SPOT **2 MORE** DIFFERENCES

It's a busy day on restaurant row,

So order some Look-Alikes "for here" or "to go."

One thing you'll notice if you stroll out this way:

It's not just the menus that change every day.

FIND THE 27 LOOK-ALIKES

ZANY ZOO

Let's feed the giraffe
with the rubbery muzzle.

Where did his spots come
from? That's really a puzzle.

FIND THE **55** LOOK-ALIKES

Find the LOOK-ALIKES
that are used for sewing.

MIND-BOGGLING MOVIES

A movie and a snack would be twice as nice.

Would you like to have an order of dice?

FIND THE **50** LOOK-ALIKES

Ouch! These LOOK-ALIKES are sharp! Which are they?

A ride on the "Wildcat" might give you the chills.

Get set for a trip that is packed full with thrills.

FIND THE **37** LOOK-ALIKES

PLAYFUL PLAYGROUND

FIND THE **37** LOOK-ALIKES

At the playground,
you can play in the sand,

Or use the sandbox to
play in the band.

BONUS CHALLENGE

Bounce on your back.
Bounce on your belly.

This bouncer will get you wobbling like jelly.

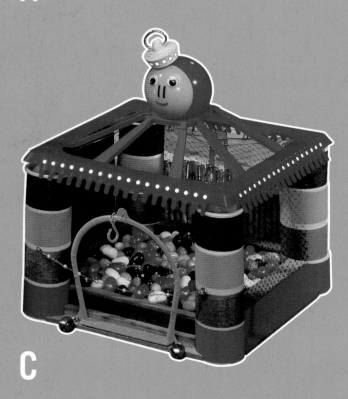

A

B

C

D

FIND THE **8** LOOK-ALIKES

Each of these bouncers
matches only one other.

Can you pair them all up,
each with its "twin brother"?

F

E

H

G

THINGS THAT GO

WHEREVER YOU GO BY LAND, SEA, OR AIR,

LOOK-ALIKES CAN HELP TO GET YOU THERE.

You won't want to miss a trick,
With this crop of Look-Alikes, ready to pick:

 Peacock feathers

 Tater Tots

 Lipstick

 Dog biscuits

 Dinosaur

 Gumdrops

 Paper clip

 Glove

 Doormat

 Pot holder

 Matches

 Hair clip

SUNNY SCHOOL BUS

The bus's tires are held on by jacks.

If they get loose, we'll all get snacks!

FIND THE **42** LOOK-ALIKES

Which LOOK-ALIKES do you use at school?

ON-THE-GO OCEAN LINER

See why the folks on deck all fled

When the captain ordered, "Full steam ahead"?

FIND THE **45** LOOK-ALIKES

Name ten LOOK-ALIKES that are also found in other scenes.

RACING ROCKET

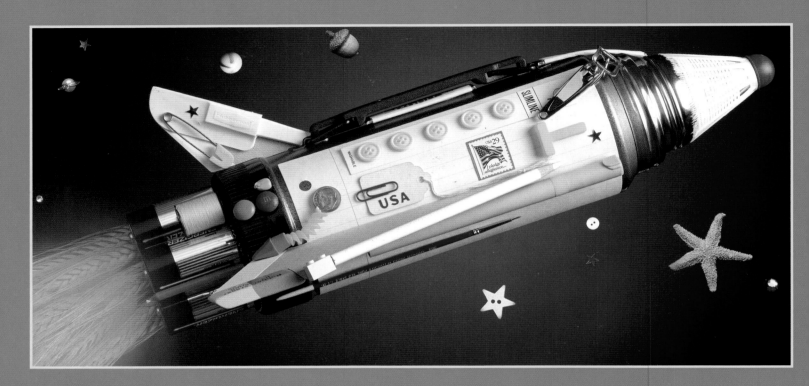

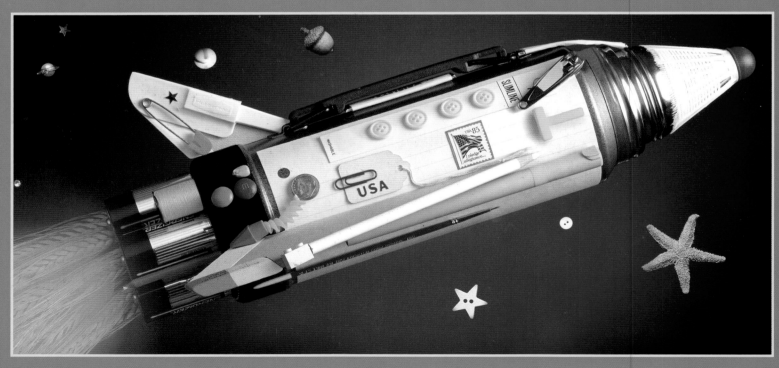

FIND THE **38** LOOK-ALIKES

Instead of "Blast off," on launching day,

"Bye-bye, Birdie" is what we say.

SNAPPY CEMENT TRUCK

For pouring sidewalks and making grilled cheese

Just call for this truck and give it a squeeze!

FIND THE **24** LOOK-ALIKES

BONUS CHALLENGE

We hope that neither spaceman forgets

The best view of Earth
is right through his jets!

FIND THE 11 LOOK-ALIKES

Although one of these spacemen is turned around,

Can all of the changes still be found?

SPOT 10 DIFFERENCES

EXTRA CHALLENGE ANSWERS

FIND ALL THE DIFFERENT EDIBLE LOOK-ALIKES. HOW MANY CAN YOU FIND? WHICH ONES ARE SWEET?
94 EDIBLE LOOK-ALIKES
Wrapped candy, candy corn, pretzel-shaped cookies, Indian corn, matzoh, pretzel, peanuts, peppermint candies, poppy seeds, bread roll, pasta twists (rotini), wrapped stick of gum, red gummy candy, jam-filled cookies, tortilla chips, cream-filled cookies, cherry tomato, lasagna noodles, slice of kiwi fruit, angel-wing cookies, fruit cookie, ravioli, tubular cookies, spinach tortilla wrapper, slice of salami, Chiclets gum, shortbread cookie, Ritz cracker, jelly beans, Cheez Doodle, breadsticks, corn kernels, chocolate bar, wrapped candy bar, Christmas cookies, shredded wheat, gummy ring, Wheat Thins, Goldfish crackers, taco shell, sugar letters, jar of peppers, cinnamon stick, Cheerio, cranberries, popcorn, slices of bread, broccoli, ice cream cone, wafer cookies, pretzel sticks, breakfast cereal, coffee beans, brownies with nuts, chopped walnuts, lettuce, two boxes of raisins, caramels, saltines, kidney beans, candy decorations, animal cracker, breadcrumbs, bread cubes, chocolate squares, Brazil nuts, hazelnuts, pasta wheels, Italian (flat) green beans, potatoes, alphabet noodles, black-eyed peas, melba toast, garlic cloves, almond, grain of rice, striped sunflower seeds, walnut halves, Tater Tots, gumdrops, parsley, M&M'S, chocolate doughnuts, peppermint Lifesaver, Triscuit crackers, pistachio nuts, fig bars, mustard bottle, peppermint stick, elbow macaroni, jar of jam, lollipop, graham crackers, bouillon cube.

COUNT UP ALL THE LOOK-ALIKES MONEY. HOW MUCH DO YOU HAVE? HOW MANY OF EACH COIN DO YOU HAVE? HOW MANY BILLS?
Total is $15.23 American dollars and 100 pesos. (Five dollar bills, eight silver dollars, two quarters, five dimes, 123 pennies, and one 100-peso coin.)

WHICH LOOK-ALIKES CAN YOU FIND IN THE WOODS? IN THE OCEAN?
12 LOOK-ALIKES
WOODS: Maple seeds, pinecones, leaves, acorns, coffee beans, acorn caps, pistachio nut, Brazil nuts, almond, walnuts, hazelnuts, cinnamon stick.
7 LOOK-ALIKES
OCEAN: Striped seashell, sea urchin shell, seashell, spiral seashell, starfish, spotted seashell, natural sponge.

FIND ALL THE ALPHABET BLOCKS. HOW MANY DO YOU HAVE? HOW MANY ARE VOWELS? HOW MANY ARE RED?
There are 46 alphabet blocks. Seven are vowels, and ten are red.

HOW MANY CRAYONS CAN YOU FIND? HOW MANY OF THEM ARE RED? GREEN? COUNT ALL THE WOODEN PENCILS, TOO.
24 crayons (eight red, six green)
57 wooden pencils

WHAT IS ONE OF THE MOST UNUSUAL LOOK-ALIKES THAT IS FOUND IN MORE THAN ONE PLACE?
The egg slicer! It's found in the DAFFY DINER and ON-THE-GO OCEAN LINER scenes.

TITLE PAGE
3 LOOK-ALIKES
CLOWN: Tiny spiral seashell, ponytail holder, tubes of paint.

COPYRIGHT PAGE
3 LOOK-ALIKES
BABY CARRIAGE: Miniature cheese, hook (hook-and-eye type), green buttons.

HAND-CRAFTED from real objects at her studio in New York's Hudson River Valley, Joan Steiner's three-dimensional Look-Alikes scenes strive to combine visual artistry with a challenging puzzle element. The award-winning Look-Alikes books have been translated into sixteen languages and have sold more than a million copies worldwide.

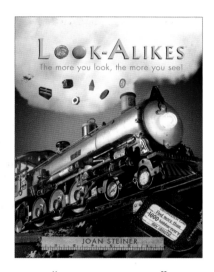

"Astounding."
—*The New York Times Book Review*

★"In Steiner's hands, the ordinary becomes extraordinary."
—*Publishers Weekly* (starred review)

"Clever, ingenious, and fun."
—*School Library Journal*

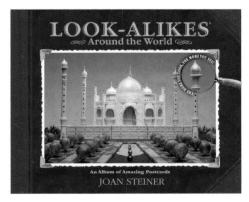

"Riveting."
—*Booklist*

To Amy and Megan,
true friends and colleagues

Little, Brown and Company

Hachette Book Group
237 Park Avenue, New York, NY 10017
Visit our website at www.lb-kids.com

Look-Alikes® is a registered trademark of Joan Steiner.
Little, Brown and Company is a division of Hachette Book Group, Inc.
The Little, Brown name and logo are trademarks of Hachette Book Group, Inc.

First Edition: July 2011

Library of Congress Control Number: 2010939617

ISBN 978-0-316-07407-0

10 9 8 7 6 5 4 3 2 1

IM

Printed in China

The illustrations for this book are photographs of three-dimensional
constructions created from found objects.
The text was set in Vinyl, and the display type is Vinyl.